MW01600833

Somebody Swiped the Stars

Lynne Buker

Illustrated by Dawn C. Shank

Copyright ©2021

Lynne Buker

All rights reserved

ISBN: 9798462316883

No part of this of this book may be reproduced or transmitted in any form or by any means, electronic or mechanical, including photocopying and retrieval system or by any information storage or retrieval system.

DEDICATION

To all the teachers I've known, especially Suzi, Tracy, Julie, Pam, Catherine, LaDawn, Lisa and 'the other' Lynn, who added love to their learning...teach on!

Preface

Jack is an All-American boy who eagerly explores the world he lives in. A typical 3rd grader, whenever he comes upon a new idea, he thoughtfully and excitedly asks questions. Join him as he searches for answers and looks to his mom to explain things and put him "in the know" and not hear "no!"

"Mom, Mom, somebody swiped the stars!" said Jack.

"What stars?" said Mom.

"The stars on our flag!" said Jack.

"Who took them?" said Mom.

"Malaysia," said Jack.

"Hmm . . . Is she someone new in your class?" asked Mom.

"No, she's a country in the Pacific Ocean," said Jack.

Smiling with understanding, Mom said, "Ah, the canton is different."

"We didn't count-on nothing. I'm telling you the stars were gone."

"You were looking at the national flag of Malaysia. That is their flag just like the one with the stars is our flag. The people of Malaysia chose symbols that mean something to them just like our stars have meaning for us," said Mom.

"Meaning *US* who?" said Jack.

"Well," said Mom. "Our stars mean the same thing to Uncle Ned in Nebraska, for Grandma Wilson in Florida, and for you and me. It is a way for all of us to think alike about our country no matter where we live."

"What symbols did you see on the Malaysian flag?"

"A sun and a moon . . . Big deal!" Jack shouted.

"They swiped the stars from OUR sky and put OUR sun and moon in its place!"

"Jack, you don't live in Malaysia, but for some people who do, these symbols might mean something special to them. What do you think it means to them?" asked Mom.

Waving his hands towards the sky, he said, "That they get up and go to bed like we do?"

"Not exactly, Jack. They live on an island in the Pacific Ocean on the other side of the world. The sun would be rising and setting just the opposite of us! Did that flag have as many red and white stripes as our flag?" asked Mom.

"No, and that's another thing. They have more!" said Jack. "Do they think they are better than us? There should only be 13!"

Laughing again, Mom continued, "What that means is that they have more reasons. Fourteen, to be exact, that symbolize something all Malaysian people recognize as *a reason for being,*" said Mom. "Being?" Jack, thinking quickly, replied. "So, they like *being* a Malaysian, like — I like *being* an American?"

"Exactly, Jack," said Mom. "We use a lot of symbols that tell everyone we are Americans, so people all over the world can understand who we are."

"Like what symbols?" said Jack.

"What do you think of when you put stamps on the letters to Uncle Ned?" asked Mom.

"All the times I have to write to thank him for the neat stuff he sends me," Jack said.

Mom giggled, "No, no, not that. What's *ON* the stamps?"

"Sometimes a bird or flower, but a lot of faces of people I don't know." said Jack.

Sighing deeply, Mom said, "OK, OK, even if you don't know them, aren't you sure they are special to Americans?"

"You want me to say yes, don't ya Mom?"

"Yes, dear. I want you to see that symbols of any country are everywhere in their land."

"Where is your lunch money?" asked Mom.

Digging in his pocket, Jack said, "You're not changing the subject on me, are you Mom? I have a nickel, a dime and two pennies. They don't have any stars or stripes on them."

Pointing to the coins, Mom said, "But they do have symbols that have special meaning for Americans."

"These coins say who we are. If you tried to use our money in Malaysia, they would think you are probably an American. You would not be able to buy anything with those coins. They have their own money just like we do. It sets each of us apart, but special, in our own way of thinking about ourselves," said Mom.

Smiling with new understanding, Jack asks, "So, if I decided I didn't want to be an American anymore, I'd have to give up our flag, stamps and money?"

"Among other things, yes," Mom said. "The reason you study other countries is to learn different ways of life and different customs that have special meaning for them. Those things are sometimes different, but make them feel they are united, just like us."

National symbols of the United States and Malaysia

US National flower — American rose

American Bald Eagle

Malaysian Tiger

Malaysian National flower — Bunga Raya

Washington, D.C. is the capitol of the United States. (Lincoln Memorial, Washington Monument and the Capitol Building)

Kuala Lampur is the capitol of Malaysia. (Petronas Tower)

Jack said, "If I went to live in Malaysia, I'd have to like that they swiped our stars for a moon and a sun?"

"Well, that's true, in a way," Mom said. "You can love many countries. If you tried to make them question what they love, they might feel disrespected. You might believe Americans have the best flag, stamps, money, and way of life. But if you started to make them think they swiped the stars, and that they should think like you . . . you could even start them fighting with each other!"

"Kind of like when I tease Jacob because he calls his church a synagogue and his minister is a rabbi?" Or I tell him the only place you can have a God is in a church with a minister?"

Wearily Mom replied, "Jack, quit teasing Jacob. You're getting the picture. He is still waving the same flag, spending the same money, and using the same stamps. Even more than liking his synagogue, he likes being an American just like you."

"What country are you studying next?"

"Zim-bob-wass and Kaboom!" said Jack.

"Zim-who and Ka-what?" Mom happily giggled.

"Jack, this is going to be a fun and exciting
school year!"

Jack's Vocabulary

Being: somebody's nature or character

Canton: a rectangular shape in the top left corner of a flag, next to the staff

Country: a nation or state that is independent and remains separate in some respects

Different: a state of being unlike others

Rabbi: the leader of a Jewish congregation

Reason: a cause for acting or thinking in a particular way

Special: being different from what is ordinary or usual

Swiped: to take something, usually with a snatching motion

Symbol: an object, character, picture, icon or motion that can represent something else

Synagogue: a place of worship of a Jewish congregation

United: what is formed by the union of two or more people

FLAG FACTS

Jack knows his American flag has 13 red and white stripes that represent the original 13 colonies that became the United States. He also knows that each of the 50 stars on the canton represents each state in the USA.

The Malaysians' crescent moon symbol represents Islam, the state religion. While not a sun at all, the 14-point star, known as the Federal Star, represents the original 14 territories that united to become Malaysia.

Acknowledgements

No author will look to publishing a manuscript that isn't, in their opinion, great. Likewise, no artist will call any creation 'perfect' that does not lend itself to reflection and comment. When you collaborate on a project like this, you need a great team to review and enhance what we thought!

We gratefully acknowledge the time and effort they spent to help make this book a wonderful addition to your personal library. A combination of friends, family, teachers and children, these folks are: Annie and Susan, Suzi, Melissa, and Margene, and our young friends, Samantha, Hailey and Griffin.

Many thanks to Dr. Tim Mounce, who guided us through this process with countless emails, hours . . . and much humor.

Somebody Swiped the Stars is a delightful encounter a small boy has when seeing the differences between his American flag and the Malaysian flag. His mom helps him to expand his thinking into all the things that symbolize his American customs and way of life with those in Malaysia.

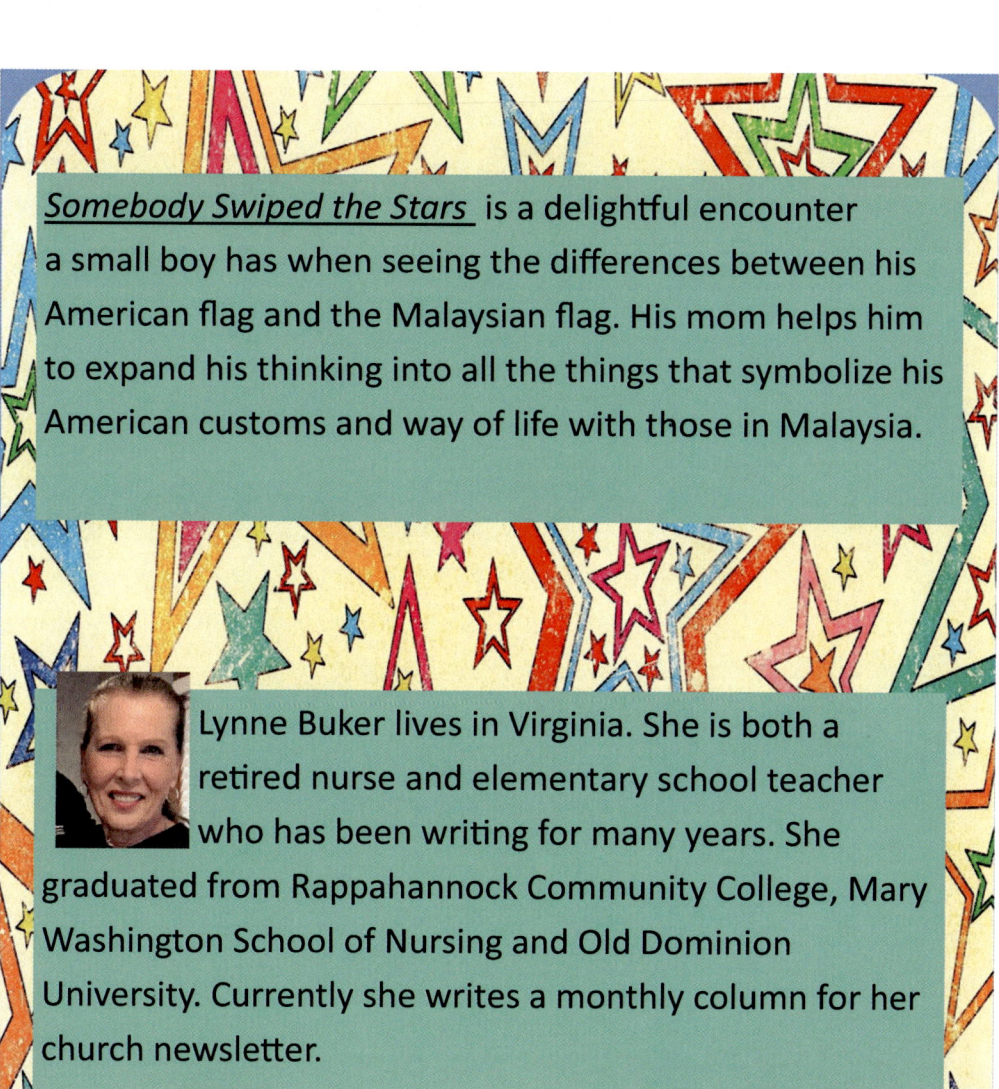

Lynne Buker lives in Virginia. She is both a retired nurse and elementary school teacher who has been writing for many years. She graduated from Rappahannock Community College, Mary Washington School of Nursing and Old Dominion University. Currently she writes a monthly column for her church newsletter.

Dawn Shank is a retired art teacher and library story time lady with a B.A. in Art Education from UNC-Greensboro. She wrote and illustrated **Raindrops Keep Falling on your Head** and **Watershed Connections**. She also writes books for her grandchildren.

Made in the USA
Middletown, DE
16 March 2023

26739166R00015